# THE BEST OF

# MAC 2012

## Cartoons from the *Daily Mail*

Stan McMurtry **mac**
*Edited by Mark Bryant*

PORTICO

**For Val Singleton, with thanks for her amazing matchmaking skills**

First published in the United Kingdom in 2012 by
Portico Books
10 Southcombe Street
London
W14 0RA

An imprint of Anova Books Company Ltd

ISBN 9781907554612

A CIP catalogue record for this book is available from the British Library.

10 9 8 7 6 5 4 3 2 1

Printed and bound by Bookwell Ltd, Finland

This book can be ordered direct from the publisher at
www.anovabooks.com

# Preface

2012. Gloom and doom everywhere. Prices up, wages down,
rising unemployment, politicians with inventive expenses demanding
that bankers stop their fiddling and so on and so on …

What should *we* do?

OK, here's a clarion call from me …
STEP FORWARD THE NATION'S CARTOONISTS!
PICK UP YOUR PENS AND DRAW! GO FORTH AND
CHEER UP YOUR COUNTRY IN THIS HOUR OF NEED.

Well, at least I've tried. I do hope the following pages will raise a smile or two.

Shortly after Rupert Murdoch's *News of the World* closed in the wake of the phone-hacking scandal it was revealed that the paper had paid a corrupt Royal Protection Officer for highly sensitive details about the Queen, her close family and staff.

'That reminds me. Charles called but the new line was a bit faint so I've no idea what he wanted.' *13 July 2011*

The British Open Championship began at Royal St George's Golf Club in Sandwich, Kent, with Northern Ireland's Rory McIlroy, winner of the US Open, a firm favourite. Meanwhile, a single ticket-holder won a record £161 million in the EuroMillions lottery.

'Don't tell me. Let me guess – Rory McIlroy has got another birdie.' *14 July*

In the wake of the phone-hacking scandal, David Cameron finally agreed to a full judicial inquiry into press standards, regulation and ownership, as well as police corruption, to be headed by Lord Justice Leveson, Chairman of the Sentencing Council.

'Full means full, sunshine. Now what devious mobile-phone wizardry were you up to on the evening of 4 July 2010?' *15 July*

After the resignation of Britain's top policeman, Commissioner Sir Paul Stephenson, over links with the *News of the World*'s editor, Neil Wallis, the paper's owner, Rupert Murdoch, faced an inquiry by a Parliamentary Select Committee.

'Don't worry, Mr Murdoch. It'll only be a few simple questions.' *19 July*

A court in Bridgend, North Wales, fined a man £2000 for fitting an electric collar to his pet dog which delivered a shock whenever the animal approached a fence surrounding his house.

'Actually, the electric collar was bought for our dog. But it's useful if Henry's sermons go on too long.' *20 July*

The leaders of 17 Eurozone countries met in Brussels in a desperate effort to break the deadlock over a second bail-out to save Greece's bankrupt economy.

'Good news, Brussels. A Brit has helped save our economy – I just got a half-euro tip.' *22 July*

The results of the Government's much-derided nationwide 'happiness survey', launched in November 2010, were published. Predictably, the subjects that mattered most to people were health, family and relationships, work, the environment and education.

'Question six. Woke up feeling slightly gloomy but later on suddenly felt really cheerful...' *26 July*

As the conflict in Libya escalated, Foreign Secretary William Hague announced that Britain had dropped its demand that the country's deposed leader, Colonel Gaddafi, should leave. Meanwhile, the whereabouts of the former dictator were still unknown.

'Yeah. That's if they can find him – sausage, egg and chips twice please, mate.' *27 July*

A survey carried out by the Department for Work & Pensions prior to the introduction of a new Employment & Support Allowance revealed that only 7 per cent, or one 1 in 14, of current Incapacity Benefit claimants were genuinely unfit for work.

'Oops. Did I say fit? – What I meant was chronic arthritic unable to walk without crutches.' *28 July*

As the war in Libya continued, President Assad of Syria sent tanks into the battered city of Hama where protests against his rule had raged for several months. However, unlike the similar situation in Libya, the West were not keen to be involved.

'Que Syria, Syria. Whatever will be, will be...' *2 August*

Despite last year's successful 'Banish the Bags' campaign by the *Daily Mail*, a survey revealed that there had been an increase in the number of plastic carrier-bags littering Britain's coastline, blighting beaches and harming marine wildlife such as seagulls.

'Remember your training, Quigly. It's, "Does madam wish for a plastic bag?"
Not, "Now you know how a seagull feels, thicko!"' *3 August*

Amidst increasing chaos regarding the new age for eligibility for a State Pension, official figures revealed that a baby girl born this year is almost eight times more likely to reach 100 than her grandmother.

'Isn't that nice, dear? The Government is offering free bungee-jumping and polar-bear-wrestling holidays for the over-70s.' *5 August*

The shooting of a suspected gangster in Tottenham, London, together with alleged 'oppressive policing', led to widespread riots and looting in the capital.

**'Here's to more oppressive policing.'** *9 August*

There was public outrage as rioting and looting by youths spread across other metropolitan areas of Britain, including Birmingham, Wolverhampton, Manchester, Liverpool and Bristol.

**'SHOOT THE LITTLE B\*\*\*\*\*\*S!'** *11 August*

As police finally began to round up rioters the courts reflected public anger and imposed heavy sentences on the criminals. Meanwhile, the official hunting season for sportsmen opened.

'For all those anticipating some nice soft sentencing. Today is the Glorious Twelfth and you have a 30-second start...' *12 August*

An 83-year-old great-grandmother from Santa Ana, California, USA, who had a £5000 operation to improve her breasts, triggered a heated debate about the pros and cons of 'growing old gracefully'.

'They did them where they found them.' *16 August*

Research by the University of Queensland, Australia, published in the *British Journal of Sports Medicine*, claimed that every hour spent viewing TV can reduce an adult's life expectancy by almost 22 minutes.

'If you feel yourself slipping away, hand over the remote.' *17 August*

Though some argued that the sentences imposed on Britain's rioters and looters by judges were extreme, with ringleaders being jailed for up to eight years, others felt that a harsh deterrent was necessary.

'It wasn't just any old flat-screen TV he nicked – it was *my* flat-screen TV!' *18 August*

Heavy-drinking, 62-year-old French film star, Gérard Depardieu, was ordered off a flight from Paris to Dublin when, having been refused access to the toilets because the aircraft was taxiing prior to take-off, he stood up in the aisle and tried to urinate into a bottle.

'That's a promise. As soon as he's had his nappy changed I'll get Gérard Depardieu's autograph.' *19 August*

An English university student formed a lobby group, Make Uni Fees Equal, and joined forces with human rights lawyers to attack a Scottish government decree to make English students at Scottish universities pay full tuition fees while Scottish and EU students go for free.

'Do stop complaining, Julian. You're moving to Auchtermuchty and changing your name to Angus McTavish.' *24 August*

As Colonel Gaddafi's compound in Tripoli fell to rebels, there was still no sign of the former Libyan dictator. Meanwhile, former Home Secretary Jacqui Smith was criticised for using day-release convicts, officially assigned to community work, to decorate her home.

'Hello. Who's Jacqui Smith got painting her house now?' *25 August*

Manchester United beat Arsenal in a spectacular 8-2 victory at United's home stadium of Old Trafford.

'... And when Manchester United scored their eighth goal, what did you do then, sir?' *30 August*

It was revealed that the Government spent more money per person on the Scots last year than they spent on the English, yet the Scots received free prescriptions, free long-term care for the elderly and free university education.

'Oh no! Not tartare of Kobe beef with caviar, followed by foie gras, scallops and black truffles again!' *31 August*

74-year-old actress Vanessa Redgrave lent her support to travellers in their fight against eviction by Basildon Council from a 1000-strong illegal settlement on Green Belt land at Dale Farm in Cray's Hill, Essex.

'And don't even think about movin' us on again or I'll set Vanessa Redgrave on you!' *1 September*

A 31-year-old male teacher at a school in Ilford, east London, was found guilty of unacceptable professional conduct by the General Teaching Council when it was revealed that he had moonlighted as a stripper and starred in pornographic films.

'Very nice, Mr Swindley. But our Barry was hoping to go into engineering.' *2 September*

In a blow to thousands who find their homes invaded by squatters and struggle through the courts to win them back, a London tribunal judge decreed that 'squatting is not a crime' and squatters should be encouraged to bring empty homes back into use.

'We've just moved in, Yer Honour. Can our Wayne borrow the car tonight?' *7 September*

Justice Secretary Kenneth Clarke announced that the long-standing ban on filming in courts would end in order to improve public understanding of the justice system.

'I believe his wife owns a boutique in the High Street.' *8 September*

MPs argued over whether to keep the 50 per cent income-tax rate for high earners. Meanwhile, it was announced that the jewellery collection of Elizabeth Taylor, estimated at £20 million, would be auctioned in December.

'Be brave, Lucinda. We all have to make sacrifices. So you may not be getting Liz Taylor's jewellery for Christmas.' *9 September*

Comedian David Walliams completed his eight-day, 140-mile, marathon swim along the length of the River Thames from Lechlade in Gloucestershire to Big Ben in London, raising more than £1 million for the Sport Relief charity.

'For the last time, I'm not David Walliams – I'M DROWNING!' *14 September*

At the Conservative Party Conference in Manchester plans were discussed to revive the 'Right to Buy' scheme introduced in 1980 during the Thatcher government. Under this scheme two million council houses could be sold to their tenants at discounts of up to 50 per cent.

'Well, here it is. And guess what? – From today it's ours, all ours!' *4 October*

Home Secretary Theresa May announced that illegal immigrants, foreign criminals and 'welfare tourists' would be stripped of their 'human right' to a family life in the UK. Meanwhile, new sightings of yetis in eastern Russia led to a six-nation conference and an international scientific expedition.

'We're off to the UK before they cut back on immigration and the human right to a family life.' *5 October*

To reinforce her point about the absurdities of current human rights legislation, Theresa May told the Conservative Party Conference about a Bolivian man who could not be deported because he had acquired a cat and thus could claim he had a family life in Britain.

'It's your landlady – another reporter is here to ask you about being saved from deportation by your cat. Shall I send him up?' *6 October*

The BBC announced that it would make £1.3 billion in cuts including reducing BBC1's TV programme budget by £35 million and relocating 1000 jobs to Salford, near Manchester.

'Well, that was the news – and now a joke about a parrot, a nun and a one-legged camel...' *7 October*

David Cameron's crackdown on TV pornography included a new website *Parentport.org.uk* – on which parents can complain about inappropriate TV images – and new legislation to force service providers to offer explicit sites by subscription only.

'Don't grumble, Wayne. I'm trying to protect you from viewing inappropriate sexual images!' *12 October*

Defence Secretary Liam Fox hit the headlines when it was revealed that he had invited his former best man and self-styled 'advisor', Adam Werrity, along on a number of foreign trips while he was on official Government business.

'... and guess who's coming with us on honeymoon? George's best man, the vicar, the organist, the bridesmaids and my mother.' *13 October*

Councils were accused of 'Big Brother' tactics to spy on residents when it was revealed that local officials sifted through the dustbins of 30,000 families last year, despite a Government pledge to stamp out the practice.

' "Fun-loving attractive blonde, 26. Seeks exciting bin snooper for secret liaisons behind refuse tip..." ' *18 October*

A report by the Health Service Ombudsman, Ann Abraham, revealed a big increase in the number of patients who had been removed from GPs' lists 'without fair warning or proper explanation' when they had made minor complaints about their doctor.

'Thank you, Mr Perkins. I've taken note of your complaint... Next!' *19 October*

David Cameron faced widespread mutiny by members of his own party when it was suggested that he might order them to block a referendum on Britain's membership of the European Union.

'It's believed he committed political suicide way back in 2011.' *20 October*

A Government-sponsored study reported that, in England and Wales, 2700 people a year died because they were unable to heat their homes due to spiralling energy costs. Meanwhile, police armed with 50,000-volt Taser guns cleared the illegal travellers' camp at Dale Farm in Essex.

'That's right. We can't afford to switch the central heating on. So thank heavens we've got our Tasers.' *21 October*

In a landmark ruling, Justice Secretary Ken Clarke announced a change to the Legal Aid, Sentencing and Punishment of Offenders Bill, whereby householders would now have the legal right to repel intruders using any force that was not 'grossly unreasonable'.

'She must be tired after her journey. Have you shown mother where she will be sleeping?' *27 October*

BBC TV's *Top Gear* presenter Jeremy Clarkson agreed to lift a gagging order preventing his ex-wife from claiming that they had had an affair after he remarried.

'Oh good. We're just in time to snuggle up with my ex-wife and watch Jeremy Clarkson on *Top Gear*.' *28 October*

Shortly before Remembrance Sunday the War Memorial Trust reported that thefts of metal plaques and statues from war memorials had more than doubled in the past year due to the increase in the value of copper and other metals.

**Britain 2011 – A Land Fit For Heroes** *1 November*

Markets nosedived around the world as the Greek government under Prime Minister George Papandreou teetered on the brink of collapse and there were fears that Greece might pull out of the Euro.

'It's a Mr Papandreou. How much would we offer for the rest of the Parthenon?' *3 November*

It was reported that 53-year-old comedienne, Dawn French, had lost more than six stone after separating from her husband last year. Meanwhile, the anti-capitalism protest outside St Paul's Cathedral in London continued.

'Nice, isn't it? It used to belong to Dawn French.' *8 November*

Home Secretary Theresa May admitted that she did not know how many foreign nationals may have entered the UK during a pilot scheme to relax passport checks at Britain's border controls.

'Come on, mate. You're holding up the queue here. Through you go.' *9 November*

Italy became the latest Eurozone country to face an economic crisis,
with fears that Britain might be dragged into a record recession.

'Answer the question, punk! – Are you gonna buy a copy of *Da Beeg Issue*?'   *11 November*

Silvio Berlusconi, the 75-year-old Prime Minister of Italy famed for his romantic liaisons, resigned in the face of the country's economic crisis and was succeeded by former EU Commissioner, 68-year-old Mario Monti.

'Hey. I thought you said Berlusconi had cleared his office.' *15 November*

There was a storm of protest when Chancellor George Osborne announced
that the cost of petrol would increase by 3p in January.

'Try to understand. We've got a puncture, two parking tickets and were being clamped when you started shouting:
"Read all about it."' *16 November*

The British Medical Association called for the Government to introduce a ban on smoking in cars as toxin levels from smoking in a closed vehicle can be 23 times higher that in a typical smoky bar, putting children and the elderly at risk.

'We know you're not smoking in the car, sir. But we'd still like a word...' *17 November*

Sir Richard Branson's Virgin Group took over part of the Northern Rock bank which had been nationalised four years ago. Virgin, best known for its airline business, paid £747 million for Northern Rock's 75 branches and one million customers.

'Before we discuss your overdraft, Mr Quigly, I think you should fasten your safety belt and wait till an oxygen mask drops from the ceiling.' *18 November*

As it was reported that Britain's 500 offshore wind turbines were scheduled to increase to 6400 by 2020, Prince Philip attacked wind farms as 'absolutely useless'.

'It was about midnight. A woman was rowing the boat and on board were
three corgis and an elderly man with a chainsaw.' *22 November*

There were fears of a crisis on maternity wards as statistics revealed a 70 per cent rise in births to women aged 40 or over – who require more nursing care than younger mothers – since 2001.

'I'm sorry, Mr and Mrs Farqueson. Your baby has done a runner.' *23 November*

A 16-year-old burglar from Leeds who was ordered to write a letter of apology to his victims as part of the Intensive Supervision & Surveillance Programme, showed no remorse and even took the opportunity to blame them for leaving a window open.

'Damned cheek! We've got a letter from our burglar blaming us for leaving the bedroom window open.' *25 November*

With two million strikers forecast to cause chaos for schools, councils, the NHS and border controls, Chancellor George Osborne's Autumn Statement unveiled even more austerity measures in the worst squeeze on incomes since the Second World War.

'It's not fair. If only I had a job I'd be on strike today.' *30 November*

A study carried out by Ohio State University on men and women aged between 18 and 25 revealed that men think about sex every 50 minutes while women do so only 10 times a day.

'Thank you, Miss Frobisher. Fill the bucket again and come back in 50 minutes.' *1 December*

Press photos of Germany's Chancellor Angela Merkel embracing France's premier Nicolas Sarkozy bore witness to the warm friendship between the two leaders. Meanwhile, two Chinese giant pandas arrived at Edinburgh Zoo and it was hoped that they would mate.

'It's a shame. They keep putting them together but I don't think Angela Merkel and Sarkozy will ever mate.' *6 December*

The National Audit Office revealed that the opening and closing ceremonies alone of the London 2012 Olympic and Paralympic Games, whose organising committee is chaired by Lord Coe, would cost £6.75 million per hour.

'Expensive but worth it, Seb. I'm told they can go on for hours.' *7 December*

Wonderbra introduced its deepest cleavage bra to date, the 'Ultimate Plunge' bra.

'Yes, those new Wonderbras are amazing. I bought one too.' *8 December*

Defence Secretary Philip Hammond announced that, for the first time in the history of the Royal Navy, female officers would be allowed to serve on Vanguard-class submarines, which carry the Trident nuclear deterrent, from 2013.

'Hello. Looks like the Christmas sales have started early.' *9 December*

An official report by Her Majesty's Inspectorate of Constabulary recommended the use of water cannon and plastic bullets if rioting returned to the streets of Britain and proposed the use of lethal force against arsonists who endangered human life.

'Those socks you bought for our Wayne. D'you think they'd fit me?' *21 December*

Transport Secretary Justine Greening approved a new £32 billion high-speed rail link, 'High Speed 2', between London and Birmingham which would include a 1.5 mile-long 'green tunnel' to be dug through countryside near Amersham, Buckinghamshire.

'Terrible news, ma'am. The master went in to the cellar to get a bottle of claret and got hit by the 8.42 to Birmingham.' *11 January 2012*

After three centuries of union, the Scottish government announced that a referendum on the country's independence from the UK would take place in 2014, the 700th anniversary of the Battle of Bannockburn, Scotland's most famous victory over the English.

'It's the question on everybody's lips. Do we really want to break away from that nice Mr Churchill?' *12 January*

Statistics published by the NHS Information Centre revealed that one Sussex NHS Trust only spends £2.57 a day, or 86p per meal, on its patients' food. Meanwhile, there were sightings of a big cat after the slaughter of a deer near Woodchester, Gloucestershire.

**'Actually it was me. I was ravenous!'** *13 January*

Cherie Blair, wife of the former Labour Prime Minister, Tony Blair, announced plans to set up a chain of private health clinics in supermarkets and shopping centres across Britain.

'He only came in to help with the shopping and I persuaded him to have a check-up.'  *17 January*

The French silent film, *The Artist*, won three awards at the 69th Golden Globes ceremony in Beverly Hills, California, but the show was stolen by the movie's co-star, Uggie the Jack Russell terrier, who delighted the crowd by standing on two legs and performing other tricks.

'Alas, poor Fido. I knew him well.' *18 January*

Having ruled out a third runway at Heathrow, the Government agreed to look at the feasibility of an airport built on an artificial island in the Thames estuary.

'Okay. We've been forced to move because of the high-speed rail link.
But this is cheap with great views, fresh air, peace and quiet...' *19 January*

Disgraced banker Sir Fred Goodwin, former head of the Royal Bank of Scotland which had to be bailed out with taxpayers' money, faced calls to be stripped of his knighthood.

'I hope I'm here on the day – I've never seen a knighthood revoked before.' *20 January*

In the House of Lords Church of England bishops joined forces with Labour peers and rebel LibDems – led by the party's former leader, Lord Ashdown – to derail the Government's plans to impose a £26,000-a-year cap on benefits for families.

'Another drink? That's very generous. Where do you chaps get all the money?' *24 January*

New guidelines announced by the Sentencing Council advised judges in England and Wales not to jail 'minor' drug-dealers, such as those caught with up to 6kg (30lb) of marijuana, but to hand out community-service sentences instead.

'This cannabis stuff. How long before the fun starts after you mix two kilos into a chocolate cake?' *25 January*

As official figures showed that the economy continued to shrink, Deputy Prime Minister Nick Clegg called for a cut in the income-tax threshold to help low-earners. Meanwhile, it was revealed that the true cost of the Olympics could be £24 billion, ten times the original estimate.

'Look on the bright side – we've got tickets for the ladies' synchronised swimming.' *27 January*

Stephen Hester, chief executive of the state-owned bank, Royal Bank of Scotland, bowed to pressure by MPs to waive his 2011 bonus (worth almost £1 million) as the bank had not done well. However, it was later revealed that his 2012 bonus would be £3.3 million.

'I think we're safe, folks. He's home and waving next year's bonus.' *31 January*

It was reported that the North American black squirrel population in Britain had risen dramatically in recent months and now threatened the existence of the grey squirrel, itself from North America, which had almost wiped out the indigenous red squirrel 50 years ago.

**'I have a dream...'** *1 February*

Following the revoking of Fred Goodwin's knighthood for bringing the honours system into disrepute, plans were announced to change the law so that disgraced peers such as Lord Archer and expenses cheat Lord Taylor of Warwick could be expelled from the House of Lords.

'Serves him right. I remember reading about the scoundrel when I was in jail for fiddling my expenses.' *2 February*

As arctic temperatures hit Britain, and the transport system ground to a halt, there were fears for pensioners as big increases in energy costs meant that many were afraid of turning the heating on.

'Do show a little compassion for the elderly, Bernard. Not everyone can afford their heating bills.' *3 February*

'Right. I've decided. After the Jubilee and the Olympics we slow down a bit. What d'you think, Philip?' *7 February*

Muslim cleric Abu Qatada, once described as Osama Bin Laden's ambassador in Europe, was released from prison on bail. Meanwhile, Britain celebrated Valentine's Day.

'Have another go. What else could make your blood pressure rise today apart from Abu Qatada being freed?' *14 February*

As parts of East Anglia, Lincolnshire and the South East were officially confirmed as in drought and temperatures soared, there were fears of a repeat of the summer of 1976 with standpipes in the street and the popular slogan, 'Save water, bath with a friend'.

'Ah, Mavis. Councillor Frobisher is here with some useful tips on saving water during the drought...' *21 February*

In the youngest ever officially diagnosed case of Gender Identity Disorder,
a five-year-old boy from Purfleet, Essex, suddenly began to believe he was a girl.

'Huh, they think they've got problems!' *22 February*

62-year-old Frenchman, Dominique Strauss-Kahn, former head of the International Monetary Fund, who lost his job after claims that he had raped a chambermaid in New York, admitted attending sex parties around the world.

'Parties always make me nervous. I hope the Dominique Strauss-Kahns won't think I look frumpy in this old dress.' *23 February*

The Audit Commission revealed that the NHS is paying GPs £65 for every patient on their books, irrespective of whether they have moved house, left the country or been dead for years. In total they are paid £162 million a year to look after 2.5 million 'ghost patients'.

'Wonderful news, Mr Pilbrow. You didn't die last year after all, so I can keep you on my books.' *24 February*

Sue Akers, a Metropolitan Police Deputy Assistant Commissioner, told the Leveson Inquiry into media ethics that the *Sun* had orchestrated a 'culture of illegal payments' to the police and public servants.

'I'm flattered, of course. But I'd still prefer our old cash-for-favours deal.' *29 February*

After 137 days the 'Occupy London' anti-capitalist protest outside St Paul's Cathedral in London was dispersed by police following a court ruling. Meanwhile, the Government proposed to expand windfarms despite protests by backbenchers against their huge subsidies.

'The last of the protesters have gone, bishop. But guess what?' *1 March*

'They're a ghastly pair anyway. We may get a few quid for them on eBay.' *6 March*

A huge magnetic storm on the Sun sent a barrage of charged particles towards the Earth at a speed of 600 miles per second, leading to fears that it would affect satellites, aircraft and electric power grids.

'Bernard. You've stolen the duvet again and your pacemaker is making a funny noise!' *9 March*

Former News International Chief Executive, Rebekah Brooks – who had earlier featured in the 'Horsegate' scandal when she was lent a retired police horse by the Metropolitan Police – was arrested with her husband over allegations of a cover-up in the phone-hacking inquiry.

'They've been released on bail with a warning and two horses.' *14 March*

Following the introduction of civil partnerships in 2005 David Cameron launched a 12-week consultation to open full civil marriage ceremonies to gay and lesbian couples for the first time.

'I'm extremely flattered, Podmore, but I'm already married. Now get on with the weeding!' *16 March*

The Prime Minister unveiled plans for the introduction of new pay-to-drive toll roads, claiming that the Treasury can no longer afford to keep funding improvements and repairs to motorways and trunk roads and that private-sector investment was needed.

'You heard the man, George. "Stand and deliver". This must be one of the new toll roads.' *20 March*

A report by the Royal College of Nursing said that the shortage of qualified nurses meant that many of those working in hospitals were left little time to talk to patients.

'Talk to me, dear. The nurses here are far too busy to have a chat.' *21 March*

There was a furious backlash over George Osborne's Budget proposal to cut higher tax allowances for pensioners. Dubbed the 'granny tax' it would mean that pensioners would pay the same amount of tax as those still working and could lose up to £200 a year.

'Thought you'd like to know, Chancellor. You've got a visitor. She says she's your granny.' *23 March*

David Cameron faced a storm of criticism after it emerged that he and his wife Samantha had hosted private dinners in their Downing Street flat for millionaire Conservative Party donors who paid £250,000 each to Tory funds.

'Cough, cough! That £250,000 was just for the meal, sir. Service wasn't included.' *27 March*

Planning Minister Greg Clark announced the biggest shake-up in the planning system for decades. However, many saw the proposed simplification and relaxing of current laws as a charter for developers to turn large sections of Green Belt countryside into housing estates and wind farms.

'Great news! Our bit of green belt isn't going to be blighted by wind turbines after all!' *28 March*

Motorists started panic-buying fuel after Government officials warned them to prepare for a possible national strike by tanker-drivers over the Easter period which could close up to 8000 petrol stations.

'I don't know why you're panicking so much. We've only got a mower!' *29 March*

Another of George Osborne's Budget proposals was the so-called 'pasty tax', a 20 per cent VAT surcharge on hot savouries such as pies, pasties, sausage rolls, toasted sandwiches and rotisserie chickens.

'Most people are stocking up on petrol!' *30 March*

In what many saw as a 'snoopers' charter' and an invasion of privacy, the Home Office announced plans to require all internet service-providers to keep records of all the nation's emails, messages on social networking sites and conversations over Skype in an attempt to catch criminals and terrorists.

'... so, happy birthday, Megan. Grandad sends his love and says to any Government snoopers listening: "S** off and get a proper job you nosey b******!" ' *3 April*

As hosepipe bans were introduced across southern and eastern England by Thames Water and other companies it was revealed that some of their directors were pocketing huge bonuses despite failing to repair leaks which allow 300 million gallons to be lost every day.

'More champagne, sir.' *6 April*

The Government ordered an investigation when the Patients' Association revealed that thousands of patients were being discharged from NHS hospitals in the middle of the night in order to free beds.

'Wakey, wakey, Mr Beasly. Two o'clock in the morning and we think you're well enough to go home now.' *13 April*

In the latest of a series of U-turns, the Prime Minister scrapped plans for a tax on home improvements. Meanwhile, British Olympics hopeful, Tom Daley, finished fifth in the synchronised diving final and won a silver medal in the individual event at the World Series in Moscow.

'That's Tom Daley's new diving partner. His back flips and U-turns are absolutely amazing.' *17 April*

A new 'pill-by-bike' emergency contraceptive service was launched in London to deliver 'morning-after pills' to women at their workplace by motorcycle courier.

'Sorry to interrupt – does a Reverend Hilda Harrington-Smythe work here?' *18 April*

It was reported in *Nature Communications* that researchers at Tokyo University of Science had succeeded in growing hair on bald mice using stem-cell technology, leading to hope that a cure for baldness in humans may soon be possible.

**'It's early days yet – so far we've only experimented with mice.'** *19 April*

A report by a parliamentary select committee on reform of the House of Lords recommended that it should contain 450 members, each serving for 15 years, of whom 80 per cent would be elected. It also advised that there should be a referendum before any changes are made.

'Perkins, until there are reforms of the Upper Chamber it's "Good morning, my Lord and Lady" not " 'Ow do, Sid and Vera!" ' *24 April*

In an attempt to crack down on dangerous dogs, the Government announced plans to require every newborn puppy to carry a microchip containing details of the owner's name and address which would then be stored in a database to which police and the RSPCA would have access.

'It's made a huge difference to my life. Instead of the dog, I had my husband microchipped.' *25 April*

With Britain on course for the wettest April on record, water companies still refused to lift the hosepipe ban. Meanwhile, to add to the 'granny tax' and 'pasty tax', the country was now officially in recession again and BSkyB (part-owned by the Murdoch media empire) looked set to lose its licence to broadcast.

'I can just about forgive the Tories for the granny tax, the pasty tax, BSkyB and being back in recession – but the hosepipe ban!' *26 April*

The Ministry of Defence revealed details of a 'ring of steel' to protect the Olympics, including jet fighters patrolling the skies of the Home Counties, Royal Navy ships stationed on the Thames and a network of surface-to-air missile batteries positioned on top of London tower blocks.

'We're proud to let you use our balcony for security during the Olympics – what's this button for?' *1 May*

Staffing problems and driving rain, combined with increased security by the UK Border Force in the run-up to the Olympic Games, led to long delays at passport control for airline passengers arriving at Heathrow airport.

'Welcome to the UK, folks. Please swim over to the arrivals building and join the queues.' *2 May*

A study by researchers at the University of Nottingham funded by the General Medical Council revealed that nearly half of all patients over 75 in Britain had been prescribed the wrong drugs by their GPs in the past year.

'Hello, Doctor Benson. Would you mind checking that prescription you gave my wife today for her lumbago?' *3 May*

The *Daily Mail* launched a nationwide 'Spring Clean for the Queen' anti-litter campaign to mark the Diamond Jubilee.

'Y'know, Mavis, I think the idea is to dispose of the litter. Not the people who drop it.' *8 May*

At the state opening of Parliament the Queen's Speech outlining the Government's
proposed reforms for the coming year lasted only 15 minutes.

'It's the Prime Minister. To cut costs next year he wants me just to do it all on Facebook.' *10 May*

Sir Michael Wilshaw, new Chief Inspector of Schools for England and head of Ofsted, the education watchdog, announced a crackdown on mobile phones in schools in an effort to improve classroom discipline and prevent cyber bullying.

'Trust me. If they do ban mobile phones in schools, you will gradually learn to speak without one.' *11 May*

Ashleigh Butler, a 17-year-old schoolgirl from Wellingborough, Northants, and her six year-old male crossbred dog, Pudsey, became a sensation after winning the final of ITV's *Britain Got Talent* with an act that including the dog dancing on its hind legs with its owner.

'I must say this is a lovely surprise, Fluffykins. It's years since anyone asked me for a dance.' *15 May*

It was announced that, to help cope with increased transport congestion, tens of thousands of Whitehall civil servants would be allowed to work from home for seven weeks during the Olympic games.

'For heaven's sake, Marjorie, dear! Can't you see I'm trying to work?' *17 May*

While accompanying the Queen to Bromley in Kent as part of her Diamond Jubilee tour of Britain, Prince Philip, noticing a 25-year-old blonde woman in a red dress with a full-length frontal zip, remarked to a policeman: 'I would get arrested if I unzipped that dress!'

'That's disappointing. He didn't say anything about unzipping dresses.' *18 May*

Only hours after the Olympic flame arrived in Britain and began its 70-day journey around the country some of the 8000 torch-bearers put their torches up for sale on eBay with prices up to £100,000.

'I've booked three weeks in the Bahamas, Ron, love – how much did you get for it?' *22 May*

Home Secretary Theresa May announced plans to scrap the Asbo (Anti-Social Behaviour Order)
introduced by the Labour government in 1998 as it had become a 'badge of honour'
prized by young thugs.

'Life's so unfair. Just when he was in line for his 100th Asbo, they've stopped them.' *23 May*

A 42-year-old ex-paratrooper and film stuntman became the first person to jump out of a helicopter at 2400 feet and land safely without a parachute. Wearing a special sail-like 'wingman' suit he glided down onto a pile of cardboard boxes in a field in Marlow, Buckinghamshire.

'I told your mother how she could save the taxi fare from Heathrow.' *25 May*

Web giant Google faced an inquiry from the Government's data-protection watchdog into claims that it had used its 'Street View' photo-mapping cars to deliberately harvest information from emails, photos and documents stored in millions of UK wi-fi home computers.

'About that email you just sent to your sister. I think I can help – have you tried hot lemon and yoghurt for your piles?' *29 May*

The Office of Fair Trading revealed that unscrupulous dentists were duping patients into paying for private treatment which was available for free on the NHS.

'Nurse. Mr Brinkly has chosen to go NHS. Mix up some Polyfilla, will you?' *30 May*

The Queen celebrated her Diamond Jubilee with four days of televised events beginning with the River Thames Jubilee Pageant featuring 1000 boats from around the Commonwealth, the largest flotilla seen on the river in 350 years.

'OK, team. I've done my bit. Now who's going to volunteer for the Ceremonial Day and the RAF fly-past?' *5 June*

As Prince Philip was taken ill after the river pageant the Queen was unaccompanied at other Jubilee events, including a concert outside Buckingham Palace, an RAF flypast, a fireworks display, the lighting of a beacon, a service at St Paul's Cathedral and a number of state receptions.

'First visit and all she said was "Move over" ' *6 June*

Home Secretary Theresa May unveiled tough new laws to make forced marriages a criminal offence in England, Wales and Northern Ireland.

'Remember back in 1954 your father saying if I didn't marry you he'd get his shotgun out?' *8 June*

After having a drink in their local pub near Chequers in Buckinghamshire, David and Samantha Cameron drove back in their separate cars unaware that they had left their 8-year-old daughter Nancy in the bar alone, each thinking she was with the other.

'I hope Cameron collects her soon. She's been droning on about the Eurozone crisis for half an hour now.' *12 June*

It was announced that the design for the tableau at the opening ceremony of the Olympics would reflect 'our green and pleasant land', and would feature a cricket pitch, a lake, a ploughed field, maypoles, artificial clouds and live animals such as sheep, horses, geese, ducks, cows and goats.

'Go and explain to them that all they'll have to do is act normally.' *13 June*

*The Times* revealed that 39-year-old comedian, Jimmy Carr, who had recently lampooned tax avoidance by wealthy Britons in his show, had himself paid £3.3 million of his earnings into a low-tax scheme based in Jersey.

'I was doing well working for the Inland Revenue till one day I was caught laughing at a Jimmy Carr joke.' *20 June*

Thousands of surgical operations had to be cancelled and there was widespread disruption of medical services when NHS hospital doctors and GPs in England went on strike over reforms to their pensions.

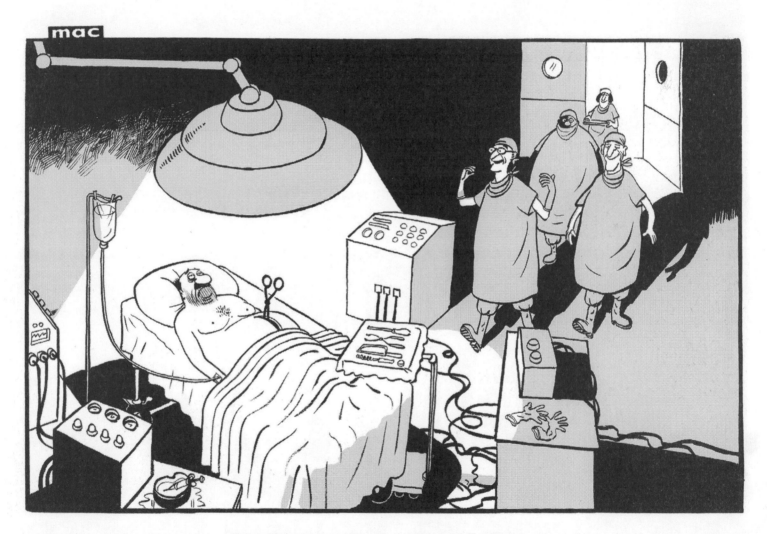

'Okay. Strike's over. Now, where were we?' *22 June*

The 30th Summer Olympics, in which more than 200 countries participated, was officially opened by the Queen. As a result London also became the first city to host the modern games three times (earlier Olympiads were held there in 1908 and 1948).

'Damn! I know I've got the key somewhere' *27 July*